INSPIRATIONAL
PAGES

Words to inspire, encourage
and cause you to look
for the good on your life's journey

Sharon C. Suggs Giesler

WESTBOW
PRESS®
A DIVISION OF THOMAS NELSON
& ZONDERVAN

WestBow Press books may be ordered through booksellers or by contacting:

WestBow Press
A Division of Thomas Nelson & Zondervan
1663 Liberty Drive
Bloomington, IN 47403
www.westbowpress.com
844-714-3454

Contact inspirational_rn@yahoo.com

Scripture taken from the King James Version of the Bible.

ISBN: 978-1-6642-6605-6 (sc)
ISBN: 978-1-6642-6604-9 (e)

Print information available on the last page.

WestBow Press rev. date: 06/06/2022

CONTENTS

INTRODUCTION

These inspirational words were written to help encourage and inspire you on your life's journey. Any encouraging or inspiring words may be helpful. For sometimes on this life journey, it can become very discouraging and disheartening. There can be some encouragement at any turn, we just don't know where it is therefore, we must keep a watchful eye and be determined to always look for the good and sure enough that is what you will find. Hope you enjoy.

COMPLAINING

What good does complaining do? The working word is good. Does complaining do any good? Have you ever stopped and taken an inventory? You have far more things to be thankful for than about which to complain. If you think about it, complaining could be listed in the devil's bag of tools. Because there is nothing negative found in God our Heavenly Father.

When you are complaining, you are not looking for the good. You are giving place to the devil as stated in Ephesians 4:27-30 (KJV).

In doing all of your complaining do remember, things can ALWAYS be worse. What does complaining do for you? If you stop and think about it, complaining make you feel worse. Complaining is negative. Does negativity improve your state of mind? Of course not. How could it? Complaining is a form of pessimism. Pessimism is looking on the dark side of things. Pessimism is the opposite of optimism. Pessimism is negative, dark side, always looking for the worst side of things. Look up and live on the optimistic or bright side of things.

What are your thoughts? Express yourself.

ARE YOU CHEERFUL TODAY?

Cheerful heart is good medicine. Proverbs 17:22 (KJV)

Are you cheerful today? If you are, please spread some of the cheer around. Everyone can use a little cheer in their lives today. As the time has been and can be so gloomy and forlorn. One can hardly hold their heads up, to make it through the day, especially since the year 2020. It was the year of the corona virus pandemic. It has been a year of gloom and doom, although there is cheer somewhere amidst all of the gloom and doom. You just have to look for the cheer, say it and believe there is cheer.

When you are cheerful, it seems to brighten your day. It makes your load seem lighter. When your load is lighter, you can move through life easier and smoother. So be of good cheer and remember to share the good cheer wherever you go.

What are your thoughts? Express yourself.

WHERE LOVE ABIDES

Where love abides, there abides God. As the bible states, God is love. I John 4:8 (KJV) Can love and hate abide at the same time in one's mind and one's thought? I dare say it is next to impossible for love and hate to abide together. It is like having light and darkness to abide together. It has to be one or the other. We have to entertain one or the other. It is difficult to have a positive thought and a negative thought at the same time. So, if we allow love to have the preeminence, things can't help but to go smoother.

We as humans are going to experience good, bad, sad, glad, ups and downs. It is up to us to choose which emotion or thought in which we want to dwell. Why not allow love to abide? It has been said that having hate is like slapping yourself and thinking that it is hurting the person or persons that you have the hate toward. Faith, hope and love, the greatest of these is love.

What are your thoughts? Express yourself.

THE BEAUTY OF THE SUNRISE

Have you ever stopped and looked at the beauty of the sunrise? Oh, such wonder. Oh, such awesome wonder. Beauty truly is in the eyes of the beholder.

As the new day dawns, you see the bright, beautiful, golden yellow sun coming up over the horizon in the east. It is absolutely gorgeous. Can you see that there truly is a God? The sun is faithful and steadfast because the sun which is a star is 93 million miles away from the earth, comes up every day in the east, not in the west, north or south but in the east. The clouds may hide the rising of the sun some mornings but it still rises. Who designed the sun, moon and stars? Not a man, only the Creator. Who is the Creator? The one and only God in Heaven. Therefore, how can anyone doubt there is an Almighty and awesome God?

What are your thoughts? Express yourself.

GOD GAVE ....

In the beginning God gave Adam Eve. In the beginning God gave Adam and Eve the plush Garden of Eden in which to live. God gave Adam and Eve all that they needed to sustain life. God gave Adam and Eve sons to love. In the beginning God gave Adam dominion over the animals and over the Garden of Eden. When Adam and Eve sinned, God once again gave Adam and Eve covering to hide their nakedness.

God gave the children of Israel a way of escape from Pharoah's army. Down through the ages, God has given and given and given. He has given the ultimate. He gave His one and only begotten Son so that we may live eternally in Heaven with Him. So now the question is WHAT HAVE I GIVEN TO GOD? Answer your question personally. Take an inventory of what have I given to God lately? Have you given Him your time, talents and or money? Have you kept all that for yourself? Have you given God time in prayer and study of His word? Have you been rushing through your daily duties and squeezing God in somewhere? Have you been giving God your scraps or have you been giving God your best? Be honest for God is a reader of hearts, let's work on giving God the best.

What are your thoughts? Express yourself.

LIGHT

Light is awesome to everyone except the devil. He does all his dirty work, mostly under the cover of darkness. Have you ever noticed that when light shines, darkness leaves? Light and darkness do not mingle together at the same time. As the scripture says, God is Light and Christ is Light. He is the Light of the world and in Him is no darkness. Do you enjoy the sunlight, the moonlight and the starlight? That reminds me, who set all these lights in motion? It is truly awesome. The morning sunrise is too beautiful. That is one of the most beautiful times of the day, the dawning of a new day. It is always a new day or a day which we have never before seen. God's mercies are new every morning. Have you ever taken the time to meditate on how important light is? The plants do not thrive as they should without light and water. By the same token, we as human beings could not thrive as we should without light, food and water. God's light should be an important part of our lives, as well as the physical light.

What are your thoughts? Express yourself.

FILL YOUR MIND WITH THE GOODNESS OF GOD

If you fill your mind with the goodness of God, you won't go wrong because you will have your mind filled with a lot of the goodness of God by which you are surrounded. There is no room for the negative and wrong. Just keep your mind filled with the positive and goodness. This may be a feat because we so often times dwell on the negative. Wonder why it is so easy to dwell on the negative? Humans always go the path of least resistance therefore we fall right into that path. Negativism is one of Satan's tricks of his trade. Here is where practice need to be exercised. If we practice keeping positive and God's goodness in the forefront of our minds we can squeeze out and leave out negativism. Remember we always have choices. So, which will you choose to practice?

What are your thoughts? Express yourself.

ENCOURAGING WORDS

Happy is the man who is filled with gratitude, therefore having a positive attitude.

Smile, for it is the language of the universe.

Love, for God is love. I John 7 (KJV). Laugh for laughter is the best medicine. Proverbs 17:22 (KJV). Be positive for it radiates to others for you know not whose life you may touch.

BE HAPPY. Always look for the good in others and everything. He who restrains his words has knowledge and he who has a cool Spirit is a man of understanding. Proverbs 17:27 (KJV) And unto man he said, Behold the fear of the LORD, that is wisdom; and depart from evil is understanding. Job 28:38 (KJV) But he who listens to me (wisdom) will dwell secure and will be at ease, without dread of evil. Proverbs 1:33 (KJV)

Give if you want to be happy as the bible says, it is more blessed to give than receive. Acts 20:35 (KJV)

What are your thoughts? Express yourself.

WHY BE NEGATIVE?

Why are we always looking and listening to the negative? Which came first, the negative or positive? Go way back to the beginning of the bible to the book of Genesis. In the beginning…. Which came first? The positive. Everything God created was good. No negative anywhere. Then came the sly serpent. Read about sly serpent in Genesis Chapter 3. He began questioning Eve. Then came the little three letter word NOT. The beginning of negativism. We have kept it alive ever since. Now if we can keep focused on the positive (which is Godly), then things can go better, be better and remain better. We just need to practice, practice, and practice some more on focusing on the positive, as practicing makes perfect. We will not be disappointed.

What are your thoughts? Express yourself.

"THE SAME GOD"

Have you ever stopped and really, truly thought about this? The God that we worship is the same God who created Adam and Eve. The same God who created the earth and everything on the earth. He set the sun, moon and stars in the beautiful blue sky. This is the same God who parted the Red Sea so that the Israelites could cross and get away from Pharoah's army. He is the same God that talked to Moses and his brother Aaron. The same God who gave Moses the ten commandments. This is the same God who instructed Noah on building the Ark. The same God whom He said that Abraham was His friend. This is the same God who shut the lions mouth when Daniel was thrown into the lion's den. This is the same God who did not allow the three Hebrew young men to be burned when thrown into the fiery furnace. Therefore, why do we feel so insignificant when God Almighty knows just how many hairs are on our heads? We must put our thoughts on the proper perspective and stop selling ourselves short. We worship the same God as they did of old bible days. Can you just imagine that?

What are your thoughts? Express yourself.

SATAN IS A LIAR

Satan is our adversary. He gets at us in our weakest area. Whatever area in our lives that we are having a problem with, you can count on Satan is after us. If there is any good thing we can say about Satan, it is that he works hard, he never gives up and he keep trying to attack us. But another thing we can count on is that Satan uses the same old tired tactics. He doesn't have anything new in his "bag of tricks". One of his main tools is DISCOURAGEMENT. He uses the same old trifling trick but it works over and over. One great piece of advice given in the bible is to **resist** the devil and he will flee from us as stated in James 4:7 (KJV) The devil can't do any more than we allow him to do. We just have to be watchful and don't fall into temptations. That is one of his tricks, he tries to attack us when we aren't looking or paying attention. The bible tells us to walk circumspect, Ephesians 5: 15-20 (KJV) which means to walk watchfully, cautiously. You are cautious in what you say and do, heeding circumstances and potential consequences thus doing all we can to avoid the snares of the old devil. He is sly, he's slick and he is cunning.

What are your thoughts? Express yourself.

TO REMAIN WITH A GRATEFUL HEART

To remain with a grateful heart, one must surely be thankful. Being thankful one surely should count their many blessings. When you stop and think about the many many things to be grateful for, you will surely remain grateful. It has been said that a thankful person is a happy person. If you are counting your blessings, you don't have much time to think about the negative things or things that get and pull you down. There are so many blessings nearby. There are so many blessings that our Creator gave to all. You don't have to meditate very long or hard to realize and recognize the blessings that we share. Our Creator has such beautiful handiwork. Look at the puffy white clouds in the beautiful blue sky, the graceful beautiful butterflies, the beautiful birds with their beautiful songs. The most beautiful colorful flowers that are awesome. Who cannot have a grateful heart with all the beauty around us?

What are your thoughts? Express yourself.

WHEN YOU ARE TRUSTING GOD

When you are trusting God, you need not fear. Believe God is always nearby. When you trust God your stress level is sure to be low. When you trust God, you are not doubting. If you are doubting, you are for sure not trusting. If you are trusting, your faith is growing. If you are fretting, you are showing doubt. There are days and times in our lives that we will stumble and fall but we don't have to lie there and wallow in our mishap of stumbling and falling. We need to pick ourselves up, with trusting God, dust ourselves off and keep marching forward renewing our trust in our God and Heavenly Father. Trust God with all your heart and lean not on your own understanding, acknowledge Him in all your ways and He will direct your paths. Proverb 3:3-5 (KJV)

What are your thoughts? Express yourself.

IT TRULY IS THE LITTLE THINGS IN LIFE

A lot of the "little things" in life are free such as the cool breeze in the morning or evenings, watching the beautiful butterflies fluttering in the air, watching the beautiful birds and especially the humming bird. They are so colorful and flutters around the flowers and the hummingbird feeders. They are amazing. If you are blessed with most of your senses, you can see the beautiful flowers, trees, hills, mountains and rock formation. If you can hear, you can enjoy the birds singing. If you are able to see, you could see the moon rising and the stars in the sky. You may be able to see the most beautiful sunrises in the east and the sunsets in the west, how awesome. Also, you may be able to see the awesome rainbow set in the sky by our Creator. Then last but not least of the "little things" is the awesome smile. You can give them away all day long and still have plenty. The smile is universal, it crosses language barriers. So put on your smile and give them away.

What are your thoughts? Express yourself.

THE SANDSTONE

The sandstone is one of God's many stone handiworks. If you are familiar with the sandstone, you know it is a "gritty" "homely" type of brown colored stone. Although the sandstone comes in a few different colors. The sandstone is a very "blasé'" "homely" ordinary looking stone. Not two stones look alike. By the same token no two people are alike, even identical twins. This is an awesome design of God. The most awesome part about the sandstone is that when it is in direct sunlight, it glistens and sparkles. It is very awesome. It shows me how God takes the "blasé'" and turn it into something beautiful. It has been said that the sandstone is a cheerful stone. One can truly say that it is true because when the sandstone is in the sun, it can bring a smile to your face. Oh, how awesome!

What are your thoughts? Express yourself.

DO YOU DOUBT GOD'S GOODNESS?

Who can doubt God's goodness? God is good all the time and all the time God is good. God is an impartial God. He is not a respecter of persons. What He does for one He can do for another. Aren't you glad that God is impartial? The bible states that God rains on the unjust as well as the just. The sun shines on us all. God is so longsuffering. He waits patiently for us to talk to Him in prayer and meditate on His Word, the bible. We can look at His Word as a love letter to us. Can you see how good God is by what He has done for us by sending His only begotten Son to die for our sins. Aren't you glad that only God can read our hearts? If you would take time out and look around, you can see God's goodness everywhere.

What are your thoughts? Express yourself.

YOU ALWAYS HAVE A CHOICE

You can choose to be happy or sad. You can choose to be uplifted or down trodden. You can choose to be glad or mad. You can choose to hate or love. You can choose to be an optimist or a pessimist. You can choose to look up or look down. You can choose to look on the bright side or on the dark side. You can choose to laugh or cry. You can choose to do good or do bad. You can choose to have a positive mental attitude. You can choose to be encouraged or you can choose to be discouraged. It is all up to you. So, what will be your choice today?

What are your thoughts? Express yourself.

EACH NEW DAY IS A "PRESENT"

Don't you like receiving presents? God's mercies are new each morning. So, it is up to you how you open your "present" each morning. You can open it with gladness, happiness and joy or regret, misery, and sadness. It is all up to you how you use your "present". Life truly is an adventure if we choose to see life as an adventure. This also is part of our "present". We don't know what is up ahead (good thing). We can explore each "present" each new day and make the most of each "present". Therefore, how are you going to open and use your "present"?

Just meditate and think about it.

What are your thoughts? Express yourself.

21 THOUGHTS

21 loving thoughts to help with a positive habit. Because after 21 consecutive days, anything done will become a habit. For the next 21 days, send loving thoughts, first to yourself. Then send loving thoughts to someone, anyone, and you can choose someone with whom you are having problems. When you send loving thoughts or kind thoughts to that person, if you can, begin in your mind to bathe that person in salmon pink color. Salmon-pink is the most calming color known. You will begin to see a difference in that person.

1. Today is still a good day.
2. God is still in control.
3. Things can be better the next hour.
4. This too shall pass.
5. God loves me and God loves you.
6. Faith, hope and love, the greatest of these is love.
7. I am special, you are special. We are special in God's sight.
8. I can make it if I try. You can make it if you try.
9. I am sending happy thoughts to myself today.
10. I am saying positive things about myself today.
11. I am thinking only happy thoughts today. I am sending you happy thoughts today.
12. Rejoice and again I say Rejoice!
13. I can do all things through Christ who strengthens me.
14. When I am rejoicing, I am not worrying.
15. When I am praying, I am not worrying.

16. All things work together for good…
17. Draw near to God and He will draw near to me.
18. Humble myself in the sight of God and He shall lift me up.
19. Be not deceived, God is not mocked. Whatsoever a man soweth that shall he also reap.
20. Seek ye first the kingdom of God and His rightness and all these things shall be added unto you.
21. Worry is doubting God's power. Matthew 6:33 (KJV)

You might want to change or add to my or all of these thoughts. Just feel free to alter them to accommodate your needs. They are just some ideas.

What are your thoughts? Express yourself.

WHY DO WE TRY TO HANDLE LIFE'S PROBLEMS AND CONCERNS ALL BY OURSELVES?

Why not allow God to handle them? There is nothing, NOTHING God can't handle. We choose not to consult God through prayer and let Him handle things. After all He knows us better than we know ourselves. What is trust? We are told to trust God. Trust is a firm belief in the reliability or strength of someone or something. Believe in the reliability, truth, ability or strength of, we can avoid much stress and anxiety if we would only trust God to handle things in our lives His way, in His time. Wonder why we can't do that readily? Wonder if we are not trusting, are we then doubting? God is bigger than any problem we can conjure up.

If we can set aside time to pray, meditate and study God's own Word daily, we would be that much better as a result.

What are your thoughts? Express yourself.

A PRAYER

Dear Father,

Help me to glorify You in everything that I do. Help me to glorify You in my daily walk. Help me to see You in my daily talk. Help me to see You in everything around me in the minutest blade of grass to the tallest tree, to the most beautiful blue sky and in all that surround me, allow me and help me to see. Please keep my mouth, my tongue, my mind and my heart from ugly guile and ugly thoughts. For as my heart, mind and soul are taken away from glorifying you, I am then allowing Satan to enter in.

Dear Father, all things that the naked eye can see is your handiwork. As we were put here to glorify You and You alone. To glorify You is to give You all the praise, glory and honor. I am to hold You dear in my heart.

In Jesus's Holy and Righteous name.

Amen

What are your thoughts? Express yourself.

WHEN THE SUN SHINES

When the sun shines, it gives us the opportunity to exercise the blessing of sight. It allows us to behold the beauty of God's handiwork.

We tend to take our blessings for granted so much. If we have a reasonable amount of our five senses that we were granted at birth, then we are very blessed.

Thank God from whom all blessings flow.

When the sun shines, we may see the free blessings all around us. If you are able to see a rainbow in the sky after the rain, Genesis 9:13 (KJV) you are blessed. If you can hear the laughter of an innocent baby or hear children playing, we are so blessed.

If only we could take time out of our busy schedule and meditate on God's goodness, we could see how we are blessed beyond all measure.

What are your thoughts? Express yourself.

BE STILL

I believe personally that the quietest and most serene time of the day is the dawning of the morning. The world has been asleep. You can hardly hear a "peep" especially on the weekends. The most awesome and beautiful sight is to see the rising of the sun. The beautiful colors of sometimes red and orange even a darkish blue when the clouds are present in the sky. You might hear the chirping of the birds in the dawning of the morning. You might see or hear squirrels or rabbits scampering around. It is so very calming and relaxing. If we could only be still long enough to slowly drink in the beauty of God's handiwork. God said in Psalm 46:10 (KJV) BE STILL and know that I AM GOD... Read I Kings 19:11-13 (KJV) it explains how God's voice came to Elijah in a still small voice.

If only we could stop, be still, listen and meditate.

What are your thoughts? Express yourself.

STAYING CLOSE TO GOD

Let us strive the rest of this year and the coming year to make our ultimate goal to get closer and stay closer to God. Let us make it our priority. We know it is difficult a lot of the time because life has set in and has basically taken over. But we must remember who gave us life in the first place. God our Father Who art in heaven. Who better to guide us in our lives than the Author and Finisher of our lives? God beckons us every day because He is longsuffering. But we tend to ignore and turn away and go on our merry way doing whatever it is that we do without giving heed to our Father. So, let us practice remembering that we are in God's presence at all times but we choose to ignore and turn away and do other things instead of being still and realizing God is with us. Deuteronomy 6:5 (KJV) And thou shalt love the Lord thy God with all thine heart, and with all thy soul, and with all thy might. So, if we are doing this, we can't help but get closer and stay closer to God. Psalm 33:1 (KJV) "Rejoice in the Lord, O ye righteous for praise is comely for the upright." Another way to stay closer to God is praising His Holy Name and rejoicing in Him. Psalm 5:11 (KJV) "But let all those that put their trust in thee rejoice: let them ever shout for joy, because Thou defendest them: let them also that love thy name be joyful in Thee." Psalm 5:12 (KJV) "For thou, Lord, wilt bless the righteous; with favor wilt thou compass him as with a shield." Also, in Psalm 16:11 (KJV) "Thou wilt shew me the path of life: in thy presence is fulness of joy; at thy right hand there are pleasures for evermore."

There are so many great and wonderful blessings in God. We just have to make up our minds and hearts that we will practice remembering whose presence we are in continually. The bible shows us we will be blessed to do this.

What are your thoughts? Express yourself.

YOUR "GOLIATH"

Are you having a "Goliath" moment in your life today? Is there something "bugging" you today or getting you down? If you are focusing on your "goliath" you are minimizing your God. I believe we all have heard the story of David and Goliath in the bible. I Samuel 17 (KJV) David was a mere child going up against a giant of a man. So how do you think David knew he could defeat that giant? It was because David knew who was surrounding him. He put his faith in who was surrounding him. So, who was defeated? Not the mere child David. So, what is holding us back from defeating our "goliath"? Maybe a trick of the devil? His biggest tool is discouragement. He uses his tool very well against us. We must remember who is also surrounding us. It is the same God that surrounded David, is surely surrounding us. We must remember He is always nearby. He is never farther than a prayer away. So do not allow the devil to have the upper hand on us and use discouragement and other tools against us. If we let the devil have the upper hand our God is entirely too small. Let's go forth and conquer.

What are your thoughts? Express yourself.

GOD IS ....

First of all, God is love. Who can deny that?

God is longsuffering.
Good is good all the time.
God is omnipotent.
God is omniscience.
God is omnipresent.
God is always nearby.
God is not the author of confusion.
God is awesome.
God is Light and in Him is no darkness.
God is wonderful.
God is compassionate.
God is the Author and Finisher of our faith.
God is the creator of everything.
God is the one and only true God.
God is the giver of life.
God is Holy.
God is trustworthy.
God is perfect.
God is merciful.
God is loving.
God is an ever-present help in time of need.
God is a refuge. We can run to Him anytime day or night.

What are your thoughts? Express yourself.

ALLOW GOD TO HAVE THE "REINS"

Allowing God to have the "reins" mean trusting Him with all you are and all you have. Allowing God to have the "reins" mean He is the pilot of your "ship of life". If you are giving Him your all and not a part or portion and you are not breaking off a piece or giving Him what is left of your life, then you are allowing Him to have the "reins". Use your life to glorify Him. We race around doing, going and give God what is left of our time, money, and talent instead of giving God off the top putting Him first in our lives. Allowing God to have the "reins" mean you are trusting God unequivocally. Allowing God to have the "reins" means less stress and strain in your life. Who knows better or who cares more than our own creator? How about practicing giving God the "reins"?

What are your thoughts? Express yourself.

COMPARISONS

Comparisons is a sure way to become unhappy. When one is comparing themselves, a person can begin to feel less than. They can start to have a low self-esteem. You are who you are. You have what you have. You can improve yourself if you choose. You can change your thinking to positive. You can count your blessing. You can be thankful for what you have and who you are. You are in control of your thinking. You can practice and practice on changing your thoughts to positive and counting your blessings one by one and focusing on becoming more grateful.

What are your thoughts? Express yourself.

YOUR QUIET PLACE

Do you have a quiet place? It is a good thing to have a quiet place. You would be able to meditate on God's goodness, collect yourself, drink in God's blessings and maybe even His handiwork. You would be able to quiet your mind and let go of some stress. As in the bible, we are told to be still and know that "I am God" (KJV).

A lot of the time we as human beings are racing around and not stopping to "smell the roses" on our life's journey.

In your quiet place, you can count your blessings. In your quiet place you can close your eyes and just relax. You might even want to day dream in your quiet place. You might want to read your bible and also do some praying. So just find your quiet place and utilize it every day.

What are your thoughts? Express yourself.

SAYING YES TO GOD

Have you ever truly thought about it? Are we constantly and consistently saying Yes to God? Did you know when we are going against what God has said and directed us to do and we don't follow directions, we are saying No to God and Yes to Satan. It doesn't seem right but if we just stop, meditate, pray and listen, we are saying Yes to Satan and No to God. When we fail to follow God's directions as laid out in God's Own Word, the bible, we are saying No to God and Yes to Satan. It seems to be easy to follow Satan without even really trying. Satan is so slick, sly, cunning, clever and tricky and we follow Satan without ever giving it a second thought. Satan is a liar (John 8:44 – KJV). To say Yes to God, we need to be on guard at all times. Don't be hasty, think, be in a prayerful attitude and be willing to listen. We can say Yes to God more often than not.

What are your thoughts? Express yourself.

PUTTING ON THE WHOLE ARMOR OF GOD

A way to say NO to the devil and Yes to God is to put on the whole armor of God. As it is stated in Ephesians 6:10-17 (KJV), "Finally my brethren be strong in the Lord and in the power of His might." Verse 11: "Put on the whole armor of God, that ye may be able to stand against the wiles of the devil." Verse 12: "For we wrestle not against flesh and blood, but against principalities, against powers, against the rulers of the darkness of this world, against spiritual wickedness in high places." Verse 13: "Wherefore take unto you the whole armor of God, that ye may be able to withstand in the evil day, and having done all, to stand." Verse 14: "Stand therefore, having your loins girt about with truth, and having on the breastplate of righteousness;" Verse 15: And your feet shod with the preparation of the gospel of peace;" Verse 16: "Above all, taking the shield of faith, wherewith ye shall be able to quench all the fiery darts of the wicked." Verse 17: "And take the helmet of salvation, and the sword of the Spirit, which is the Word of God:" Therefore with the whole armor of God we can say Yes to God and No to the devil.

What are your thoughts? Express yourself.

GOD IS AMAZING

God is so amazing – Who can fathom? God made the beautiful sky, the golden yellow sun, the beautiful green trees and green grass and all manner of color of flowers you can imagine. Do you ever stop and meditate and wonder about God's magnificent handiwork? In the autumn, who changes the leaves to gold? In the winter, who makes it snow? In the spring, who makes the beautiful flowers grow? In the summer, who makes the vegetables grow and from where does the summer heat comes? How does the birds know to sing? How does a rooster know to crow at the crack of dawn? If you stop and think about it, man has nothing to do with God's amazing wonders.

What are your thoughts? Express yourself.

DON'T GIVE THE DEVIL A HOME IN YOUR HEART

The devil is so cunning, sly and subtle as stated in Genesis 3:1 (KJV). He is trying to seek all whom he may devour as stated in I Peter 5:8 (KJV). Do we think that Satan care about us? Absolutely not! He is trying his dead level best to devour all of God's people because he knows where he is headed and he is trying to capture as many of God's people as he can. His fate is sealed. Matthew 25:41 (KJV). Satan disguises himself as an angel of light as stated in II Corinthians11:14 (KJV). Satan was thrown down from Heaven: Revelations 12:79 (KJV) and there was war in Heaven. Michael and his angels fought against the dragon and the dragon fought and his angels and prevailed not, neither was their place found any more in heaven. And the great dragon was cast out. That old serpent called the Devil and Satan, which deceives the whole world. So, let's not give Satan a home in our hearts.

What are your thoughts? Express yourself.

THE BEAUTY ON THE INSIDE

It truly is the beauty on the inside. No matter what one look like on the outside. What counts is the beauty on the inside. We as human beings usually judge someone by their outward appearance. Only God can judge the heart true enough. We should not do any judging of anyone until we get to know the person or at least talk to the person. The bible directs us to "Be not forgetful to entertain strangers: for thereby some have entertained angels unawares." Hebrew 13:3 (KJV) The bible also states to do good unto all men thereby not treating someone highly different because of what they have. We are all God's creatures. Just because we were all made from dirt does not give us licenses to treat others like dirt.

What are your thoughts? Express yourself.

WHAT IS HOLDING YOU BACK?

Now that we have the whole armor of God, we can withstand the wiles of the devil. The scripture says so. We have to be strong and hold our own. This is where our faith comes in. We can put our faith and trust in God who is the Author and Finisher of our faith. We do not have to have much faith to move mountains as stated in Matthew 17:20 (KJV)... If we have faith as a grain of mustard seed, ye shall say unto this mountain, remove hence to yonder place; and it shall remove; and nothing shall be impossible unto you. If you are familiar with a mustard seed, you know the story of the mustard seed. It is very small. It measures from 0.039 to 0.079 inches. That goes to show us we don't need a great amount of faith, just use whatever the smallest amount of faith we have and God's help. So, there should be nothing holding us back but ourselves. So, let's get out of ourselves way and allow God to work in our lives.

What are your thoughts? Express yourself.

FROM THIS DAY FORWARD

Awaken every morning, thank the Father for another night and then ask God the Father what does He want today. Not your will but the Father's Will.

When you remember to do this throughout the day, you will release yourself from stress, fret, and worry. Because you are allowing the Father to have preeminence. The Father will help you with decisions and anything else you need help with during the day. If we practice this for 21 days consistently it will become part of our daily worship without difficulty. Let us remember to do this.

Psalm 5:11 – "But let all those that put their trust in thee rejoice: let them ever shout for joy, because thou protectest them: Let them also that love thy name be joyful in thee." (KJV) Psalm 5:12 – "For thou, Lord, will bless the righteous; with favour wilt thou compass him as with a shield." (KJV) Proverbs 3:5 – "Trust in the Lord with all thine heart; and lean not unto thine own understanding." (KJV) Proverbs 3:6 – "In all thy ways acknowledge Him, and He will direct thy path." (KJV) Proverbs 3:7 – "Be not wise in thine own eyes: Fear the Lord, and depart from evil." (KJV) Proverbs 3:13 – "Happy is the man that findeth wisdom, and the man that getteth understanding." (KJV) Proverbs 16:7 – "When a man's ways please the Lord, He maketh even his enemies to be at peace with him." (KJV) Psalm 136: 1 – "O give thanks unto the Lord; for He is good: for his mercy endureth forever." (KJV) Psalm 136: 2 – "O give thanks unto the God of gods: For His mercy endureth forever." (KJV)

What are your thoughts? Express yourself.

PSALM 119:105

Psalm 119:105 (KJV) Thy word is a lamp unto my feet, and a light unto my path!

Would you think the reason why so many of us are lost and groping in the dark is because we fail to consult and use God's Own Word? The bible as the scripture said, the Word is a lamp unto my feet and a light unto my path. If we are utilizing the Word, we wouldn't be in the darkness and wondering around in darkness. Jesus is the Light – John 8:12 (KJV). So, if we allow Jesus to be a Light in our life, we will not walk in darkness. So, if we study and meditate on God's Word, we will be guided by the Light.

Who wants to be in darkness especially when we can be in Light as He is in the Light? When the Light is on, darkness has to leave. Therefore, let us walk in the Light as He is in the Light.

What are your thoughts? Express yourself.

THE AWESOME RAINBOW

Who cannot be held in awe of the rainbow? This is a phenomenon of God the Creator. Have you ever saw a rainbow after a rain or storm and the sun shines against the clouds? The rainbow is so awesome. The beginning of the rainbow is recorded in the bible in Genesis 9:13 (KJV). God stated I do set my bow in the cloud and it shall be for a token of a covenant between Me and the earth. Verse 14: "And it shall come to pass, when I bring a cloud over the earth, that the bow shall be seen in the cloud. Verse 15: And I will remember my covenant, which is between Me and you and every living creature of all flesh; and the waters shall no more become a flood to destroy all flesh. So, as you look in the sky after a rain and the sun is shining you may see a beautiful rainbow and you may surely say that God is remembering His covenant with man.

What are your thoughts? Express yourself.

THE WIND

The wind is another one of God's awesome creations. The wind cannot be seen, smelt, or tasted. The wind can be a gentle breeze or it can be a horrific hurricane or tornado which can be very destructive. We cannot see the wind but we can see the effects of the wind. We can see the leaves of the trees sway. We can see the waves in the water as a result of the wind blowing. The wind was used to produce electricity. The wind can blow up a cool summer breeze which can be so relaxing and calming. The wind on the other hand can blow up a cold winter blizzard. The wind can be such a positive thing and it can be such a negative thing. However, no matter what, the wind cannot be held or harnessed. It is one of God's unexplained awesome handiworks. God used a strong east wind to part the Red Sea for the children of Israel to cross on dry land to escape the Egyptian army. Another awesome miracle of God the Creator.

What are your thoughts? Express yourself.

BITTER WITH THE SWEET

Sometimes do you ever wonder why you have to experience the bitter with the sweet? Sometimes it might be to help us to appreciate the sweet after going through the bitter. After all, look at the rose. The rose is such a beautiful flower yet the thorns on the rose are unpleasant if you are stuck by the thorn. Another example is the blackberry bush, the blackberries can be ever so sweet and delicious but in order to get to the blackberries you may encounter a thorn. In order to see the beautiful rainbow in the sky there must be some clouds, rain and maybe even a storm but it would all be worth it to get to see the beautiful rainbow in the sky. One of the most miraculous bitter with the sweet encounter is the pain of birth. This pain is almost the worst pain a woman can endure but when it is all over the most precious little person comes into the world, it was all worth the pain suffered.

What are your thoughts? Express yourself.

THE THORN TREE

Are you familiar with the thorn tree? The thorn tree although one of God's creations, "it can be a thorn" in your side. (no pun intended) The thorn tree or thorn bush, I would venture to say that is where the ones who placed a crown of thorns on Jesus's head got them. If you have ever seen a thorn tree, the thorns are pointed, stiff and painful. The thorns do not bend. The thorns are vicious. If you ever encounter a thorn tree, you want to be very, very careful because a thorn is not forgiving. The thorn puncture is very irritating. If you would meditate on the pain that the thorn inflicted on Jesus, it could move you to tears for you would have a mere taste of the pain that Jesus endured just for you and me. Can you even imagine the pain and agony that Jesus suffered? Can you imagine the crown of thorns placed on Jesus's head?

What are your thoughts? Express yourself.

PAYING IT FORWARD

Most everyone has heard of the phrase pay it forward. This is a rewarding act. The one that pays it forward gets the most reward. Personally, speaking I have been on both ends of the spectrum. For an instance, my husband and I were at a foot massage shop in New Orleans, Louisiana. We were just enjoying our foot massage but when we were about finished one of the massage therapists informed us that our massages were paid. We were overjoyed and couldn't believe that had happened. A couple who had just finished getting a foot massage paid for our massages and one other person. We didn't get to thank the couple as they had left the shop. That put a big smile on all our faces. On the other end of the spectrum, I had paid an older lady's electric bill for her, unbeknownst to her. She was surprised but I don't think she knew to this day who paid her bill. When one pays it forward without announcing what you did it is so much more rewarding. There used to be a time that random acts of kindness were in the "limelight". It was a good thing then and it is still a good thing now. I have sent someone a thinking of you card with a $10 bill inside anonymously. Although it is not recommended to send cash through the mail. Just doing any little random Act of Kindness without seeking praise is always a good thing. If someone offers to do an act of kindness for you just accept it, thank them and appreciate them because if you refuse, you might be blocking their blessings. I would venture to say if there were more random acts of kindness practiced, this world might be a little better place.

What are your thoughts? Express yourself.

First of all, I want to give God all the glory, honor and praise due Him. I want to Thank Him for those words! I want to thank my sister Renee Kindle for helping me with getting the words set properly on the pages.

I would like to thank you very much for reading this book Inspirational Pages. Hope you were able to glean much good from these words. Hope you were able to glean some encouragement and some good thoughts to help you along your life's journey.

Printed in the United States
by Baker & Taylor Publisher Services